THE
EXCITING CHURCH

where people

really

pray

THE EXCITING where

CHURCH

people
really
pray

CHARLIE W. SHEDD

Word Books,
Publisher
Waco, Texas

To Tom and Louise—thank you

Contents

Introduction

Sorry about those empty pews. Too many places. Big church, little church, miscellaneous sizes in between. City, town, open country. Pews built for people, but nobody in them.

Yet the real tragedy of the church is not those empty pews. It's empty people.

I'm invited often to church groups of every size and all denominations. Elite. Middle of the road. Right. Left. Blue collar. White collar.

This gives me a good look at what's going on in the church. And I see some positive changes. One is that denominationalism is dying. For most people these days labels aren't what they used to be.

Neither is size. "Jumboism" has had it too for many people. They seem to be wanting the personal, the intimate.

This book is about a prayer experiment in a little southern church. Jekyll Island, Georgia, is nine miles long, one mile wide, and eight miles out in the ocean. Limited as we are, we'll never set numerical records at Jekyll Island. Which means, naturally, that our only challenge is to be effective within limits.

Ours is a resort area. Because we are easily accessible by causeway, more than three million visitors come our way annually. They drive across the Marshes of Glynn to golf on beautiful fairways. They fish, sleep in the sun, walk our white beach. Many of them come to church. Summertime they worship under the big oak.

After service, they stay for coffee and a visit. They like that. Some of them come from churches without much warmth. Perhaps our *Welcome* hanger on their motel door prompted their attendance. Maybe it's simply that they have time to think now. For whatever reason, they crowd our sanctuary and overflow into the mission's parlor.

So it's an exciting congregation in its own small way. Limited by geography as we are, we'll never be a growing membership. Our only hope is the excitement from genuine growth in things of the Spirit.

The story you are about to hear is true. It is the account of people and prayers and how one little church got

turned on. From deep sleep to genuine awakening is a thrilling account anywhere it's happening. And I believe the same miracle can take place in any church where people really pray. Names have been changed in respect for individual privacy. But the folks are real and so is the "turn on."

In the first chapter I'll tell you a little of my own background. I think the picture will be clearer if you know something of my personal prayer experience.

I

The Church's First Business

1

Minor Prophet—Major Question

Question: What is the first mark of an authentic church?

Until we moved to Houston, Texas, I had given that question very little thought. I had been in some prestigious pulpits. Now I had come to sit in a pasture. We were starting a new congregation. There was a beat-up house for our first meetings. It was little. It was old. Yet because it was on a strategic corner, the people came like crazy.

I had been called to this interesting spot because I'd been successful as a churchman. I had written for denominational magazines and they invited me to speak on my ideas. But something was lacking. Inside I wasn't so sure about all my fine concepts and the authentic church.

So I was ready for a retake at that first meeting of our board. One of our young officers stood and laid it on us.

"What do you all think Christ wants this church to be?" To find our answers we decided on an interesting study. We would take a red-letter edition of the New Testament and "deep think" the words of Jesus.

At the next meeting came another question boring in hard on the first: "I wonder what would happen in our congregation if every member was prayed for every day by someone?"

That from Don. Contractor. Young father. Officer in the new church. He'd be the first to ask, "What am I doing on a church board?" Don didn't know much theology and zero ecclesiastical protocol. But he wanted his church to be what the Lord wanted it to be.

So that night he stopped us in our tracks when he asked, "Is this the most specific thing Jesus said about his church, 'My house shall be called a house of prayer'? I really wonder what would happen if everyone in our congregation was prayed for every day by someone."

Naturally, they looked to me for guidance. And I never in all my life felt so much like a minor prophet. The pulpit committee had drilled a dry hole and the board was finding it out. They knew I had no answers and I knew it.

That's a puny background for writing a book on prayer in even a little church, isn't it? But I thought in all honesty you should know how it *was* before you know how it *is* at Jekyll Island.

Of course, I had prayed in my ministerial duties. I had prayed at church, hospital beds, athletic contests, service clubs, conventions. Plus I had an adequate repertoire of prayers for meals in the homes of the parish. But for leading a praying church, this little group had drawn a blank.

Since there was no place to go for help, we decided to dig it out ourselves. We would study prayer. We'd get the people to study with us.

Some way we would find answers.

I struggled, and my people did. Sometimes we wound up in left field. Sometimes in right. Sometimes in spaces too far out for our minds to handle. And along the way, we came to some all-important realizations. One of these was the basic truth that *prayer is not first man's trying to get through to God. It is first an opening up to God who is trying to get through to us.*

If you already knew that and are shocked by my kindergarten level, don't turn me off. It sounds so elementary, doesn't it? And it is. But since that day, I have found plenty of company down this road. Thousands, clergymen included, think of prayer first as reaching for a distant deity.

Of course, one kind of prayer *is* reaching. But the first concept for great prayer is to know that God is already reaching for us. I came to understand that there is no greater definition of prayer in the Scripture than Revelation 3:20, "Behold, I stand at the door, and knock: if any man hear my voice, and open the door, I will come in."

With this insight I saw my ministry in new light. My first job was not to storm heaven's gates for my people. Nor plead for them. Nor beg a reluctant God to bless us with his favors. It was to teach the opening of inner doors with the simple prayer, "Come in."

How could a young pastor or a clergyman of any age have come this far with blinders on his eyes? One answer, I think, is traceable to those seminaries that have no courses on prayer. Theological schools tip heavy to the scholastic. Hail to the intellectual. Study your doctrine thoroughly, boys. If you will put your mind to all this good stuff, you'll have what it takes.

I'm not knocking brains, nor creeds, nor beliefs that really count. But in looking back on my seminary days, I see one grave error. In teaching me to think about God, they forgot this one important truth—God is already thinking about me.

I do not think that all the church's flaws can be traced to seminaries. But I do believe that tomorrow's theological schools will have a new beat. In place of the heavy stuff alone, they will feature also the glad notes of celebration. And the young ministers will be trained to lead their people in this truth: God loves us so much that he continually seeks us.

This is the first secret and first movement of prayer at its best.

2

Prayer Partners

How many ministers have the experience of moving from a four-thousand-member church to one of sixty-seven?

Only one I know.

Me.

I made the move because I felt it was the thing to do. I needed more time to write, but I didn't want to sever my ties with "the church."

So we moved from one of the fastest growing churches in our denomination. And it wasn't easy, but it was exciting. Many ways.

When we had lived at Jekyll Island two months, we knew some things for sure. One was that this church must be integrated.

Our state denominational headquarters had asked for

an open-door policy in every congregation. Some had put that request on the list of tabled items for future reference. Our officers were among them. They had moved it to a corner of the table in the hope that it would go away.

Restaurants welcomed people of all races, every color. So did motels, parks, beaches, pools, and the other public places on our island. But not the church. In actuality "the church" in our community stood as the one last bastion of segregation.

So we fought that battle first. Of course, we lost some of the few members we had. When our officers voted an open-door policy, some vowed never to enter the doors again. And they haven't. That hurts, because I like to keep everybody happy. It's a weakness, but that's how I am.

Then a wonderful thing happened. For every one who went away there were several who came to take their place. In even a small community, there *are* people waiting for the church to be *the* church.

Until this time there were very few signs of life around here. Sundays only a handful came to worship. Or two handfuls, like ten. A big building debt laid heavy on the few members we had. Careful check showed forty still with us and the rest long gone.

There are three churches on Jekyll Island. Everyone says, and of course they're right, we should have only one.

Yet you know how it goes. Bishops, presbyteries, denominational high honchos had created another little tragedy. So now three churches where we should have been one. Three weak churches.

We did have eight officers and most of them interested. That was hopeful. Some old. Some not so old. Some with young ideas, and some who could qualify for that whimsical epitaph, "Come weal, come woe, my status is quo."

At one of our first meetings I had chosen this text for our meditation: "First of all, then, I urge that supplications, prayers, intercessions, and thanksgiving be made for all men" (1 Tim. 2:1).

We discussed the verse, and someone zeroed in on the "first things first" meaning. It does say, doesn't it, that prayer is the *first* business of the church?

I asked if they would join me in a thirty-day experiment. Would they be willing to pray for each other by specific assignment?

To my amazement, this was something new for every one of these men. One had been an elder in our denomination for more than thirty years. Two others had been officers of long standing in other communions.

As we considered the experiment, it was apparent that two were skeptical. Two seemed bewildered. But four took to it as a real possibility for themselves and their church. Yet all were willing to try, and I was proud of them.

So they counted off—one, two, three, four. One, two,

three, four. Then, paired by numbers, they went away to share their needs eyeball to eyeball as prayer partners.

As they came back from their half hour in various rooms, one man whispered, "I had no idea 'J' was hurting like that. He spent the whole time on his problem. I didn't even get to tell him what I wanted him to pray for."

So for thirty days they continued in this person-to-person prayer relationship. Mostly they were on their own to work it out together. I didn't check on them. I heard them visiting about it with each other after worship on Sunday. They commented or asked questions in the barbershop or at the post office. That's how I knew most of them were trying.

At the next monthly meeting we had a discussion. How were the prayer partner relationships going? Great, some places. From others, zero.

So I asked them to continue with different assignments the following month. Same method. Count off. Before the count, one man said, "No way I'm changing partners. This is the first time in six months my stocks have gone up."

You think that's a superficial reason for prayer? So do I, if that's all there is to it. But sometimes the Lord takes shallow reasons and moves them to deeper realities. He did that here. That same man in five years has become one of the real prayer powers in our church. In any event,

the next month his stocks had gone down and he was willing to change.

The third month we did it again. At this meeting one man said, "You know 'L' and I have been in business next to each other for five years. And since we've been prayer partners, this is the first time I ever cared what went on in his office. So I guess you'd have to say, even if my prayers didn't do any good for him, they did for me."

Another reported, " 'V' and I meet for coffee together. It really feels good to know that somebody is praying for me."

Now hear this!

At the end of the third month one of the original skeptics made an amazing statement, for him. It was the move which would take the prayer partner program from the board into the congregation. "You all know what happened in our family this month," he began. "When my wife went to the hospital for her operation, I can't tell you what it meant to know that 'K' and his wife would be praying for her every day. You know what I think? I think we should have everybody in the congregation praying. Why don't we ask *them* to pray for each other?"

3

The Move to Include All

Andy Mansen is an ex-football star. He manages a shrimp company, has a beautiful wife, two sons, two daughters.

It was an impressive day when he stood in our pulpit to say, "I've been in this church four years now. That means eight families I feel close to. I hope the Lord leaves us at Jekyll Island long enough to be prayer partners with every single family in our congregation."

Maybe it was impressive partly because it was Andy. He's a massive man. All-everything from a school where they go for rugged football players. So somehow, hearing this big tackle witness to his prayer life adds a nice kind of excitement to the church. But there are many exciting things in our congregation. And it's been like that from the beginning.

Those first officers made a wise move which should be noted here. They asked our congregation to begin this program on an experimental basis. That has to be good, especially where old traditions prevail. Even the doubtful are more likely to accept changes on a "let's see" basis. The officers announced it several weeks in advance. This too was wise because it allowed plenty of time for questions and discussions. From the pulpit some of them told what prayer partners had meant in their lives.

Our first appointments were made at a church night dinner. The congregation was divided into prayer trios, each family assigned two other families.

We made certain that one concerned family was included in each group. These were the serious church people, those we knew would really care. I'm glad to report that five years later the complexion of our church has changed completely. It has changed so much that each trio now has two strong families. Some, three. But from the beginning, no trio was without a likely leader.*

In our particular congregation we have a large percentage of associate members. These are part-time residents of Jekyll Island. They are affectionately known as "snow birds," because they come from the north during the winter months. These too are included in the pairings.

---

*For committees and those interested in details, a question and answer section is included in Section III of this book. It discusses specifics on assigning families and deals with special problems.

Their prayer responsibility does not end when they leave our island. They are appointed for the year. Regular letters, long-distance calls keep them in touch with their prayer partners. In their case this program has proven that physical proximity is not necessary to prayer partnership.

Some of our trios meet regularly. One group monthly for dessert. Another gets together quarterly at a local restaurant. Picnics on the beach. Weekend camping. Sailing. Fishing. Golf. Tennis. And an endless variety of closeness.

We do not ask prayer partners to do these things. The only pressure applied for togetherness is what the Lord puts on them through their prayers. Some won't want close personal contact. Others don't need it. And some become very effective as prayer partners without much social contact.

4

Myriad Ways

"The proper way for a man to pray,"
    Said Deacon Lemuel Keyes,
"And the only proper attitude
    Is down upon his knees."
"No, I should say the way to pray,"
    Said the Reverend Doctor Wise,
"Is standing straight with outstretched arms,
    And rapt and upturned eyes."

"Oh, no, no, no," said Elder Snow,
    "Such posture is too proud;
A man should pray with eyes fast closed,
    And head contritely bowed."

"It seems to me his hands should be
    Austerely clasped in front,
With both thumbs pointed toward the ground,"
    Said Reverend Doctor Blunt.

"Last year I fell in Hidgin's well
    Head first," said Cyrus Brown.
"With both my heels a stickin' up,
    My head a-pointin' down;
An' I made a prayer right then an' there—
    Best prayer I ever said,
The prayingest prayer I ever prayed,
    Was a-standing on my head!"

Sam Walter Foss

"Country" poetry may not always satisfy the requirements of good literature. But sometimes it gets the point across loud and clear. And the point here is that elasticity is a must for local church prayer programs.

There *are* myriad ways to pray. This is why we sound the note—"We challenge you to pray *your* way. We tell you how others do it. But we encourage you to discover your own time, your own place and method."

The infinite variety of approaches to prayer can best be described from where it's happening. Here from actual reports of praying people, I have chosen vignettes. They

illustrate both the simple beauty and the wide scope of
individual response.

"Interesting things" at our house is the main feature
of family devotions. Every evening at dinner each member describes his favorite moment of the day. One night,
when he was eleven, Tim told this story. Tim is our
youngest.

He and Dr. Porter were going to see Duffy. Duffy
attends a private school three hundred miles away. Duffy
is also Dr. Porter's son and Tim's good friend.

As they approached the bridge leading off our island,
the doctor turned to his passenger and said, "Now, Tim,
every morning when I cross the causeway I do my praying. By the time we reach the main highway, I'll have my
prayer partners prayed for, and then we'll have a good
visit. If you want to, you can do your praying now too."
So they did, silently.

That was Tim's interesting thing and it was beautiful.
Driver and boy praying together across the Marshes of
Glynn.

Lots of people in our church make a chapel of their
cars.

Julie is the kind anyone would like for a prayer partner.
She is the mother of three boys. Handsome guys! But,
Lord have mercy, are they normal! Any one of them could

qualify for the all-American accolade: "He's a pistol!"

If you were to ask Julie when she does her praying, she'd take you to the kitchen sink. There on the window ledge are the names of her prayer partners. For Julie, the getting of meals and doing of dishes is a time to talk with the Lord.

Guy is a high school coach. He says, "I do my best praying in the shower. Since I shower every morning, it's a great time for me. You know, getting myself all freshened up is a good time to think of others. And there aren't many interruptions there. So I just shower away until I have my prayer partners prayed for. You think that's O.K.?"

Of course, it's O.K.

The Hamiltons pray together for their prayer partners every morning after breakfast. They have time then. You can do things when you're retired and on a different schedule. They say it's a great way for them to start the day.

Lawrence does his praying first thing in the morning as he watches the sunrise.

Tom likes noonday. He sits on a bench overlooking the ocean. The waves coming in and going out make for good praying.

Grandma A. keeps a list in her Bible. It's a list of people for whom she's praying, including her prayer partners. For her, it's all part of her daily devotions.

Ronnie says it's best for him when he goes to bed. He's a high schooler. Like the other students of our church, he has his daily prayer assignments.

Dave runs an employment office. Every day at noon he gets back from lunch and prays first thing.

Sue sells women's clothes. She likes to pray for her prayer partners while she's waiting on customers. For her that's a good time to talk with the Lord.

It says in the Book that there are twelve gates to the Holy City. In any effective prayer partner program there will be as many different ways to pray as there are people.

If you were a member of the Jekyll Island Church, there would be plenty of prayer training for you. Often the sermon at morning worship focuses on prayer. We study some biblical passage where someone got through to the Lord for sure.

For those interested we schedule meetings to discuss prayer, listen to a guest speaker, share ideas. At these events the praying people report on interesting results of their prayers.

Our church literature rack is filled with pamphlets and books on prayer. Funds for these are included in our budget. Sometimes memorials are given to underwrite prayer guides for those who feel the need of study. We order materials from a wide range of church headquarters and nondenominational sources.*

Some of our members are avid students of prayer. Some aren't because they pray naturally. I learned something important from the young car salesman who said, "I'm doing just fine, thank you. Don't confuse me with all your how to's."

So we encourage those who need encouragement. We guide the ones who want guidance. But through it all, we remember God is already seeking his own. And the greatest prayer is response to the Lord who is seeking us.

---

*A bibliography of books and materials used at Memorial Drive Church in Houston, Texas, is printed in *How to Develop a Praying Church*, Charlie W. Shedd, Abingdon, 1964. This book is a report of prayer activities in a large suburban congregation.

II

Where the People Pray—
These Good Things Happen

5

Where the People Pray—
They Care for Each Other

There are many pluses in our particular prayer program. But in my opinion, this is number one—an effective lay ministry. Is there any church member anywhere who ever got too much attention? Too much prayer? Too much loving care?

When Billy Sunday was America's leading evangelist, he made an interesting gesture prior to each engagement. Booked into a certain town, he would write the mayor in advance. Did the mayor know people in his community with special needs? Billy Sunday and his staff would like to be praying for them before they arrived. According to this account, the mayor of a great metropolis thought that request over and sent the evangelist their city telephone directory.

Right on!

There is no citizen of any town and no member of any church exempt from the need for prayer.

What does a person have a right to expect when he joins the church?

He has a right to expect:

> Inspiration from worship
> Mental stimulation from the sermons
> Fellowship
> A place where he can serve the needs of others.

But doesn't he also have a right to expect that someone will be concerned about him?

In New Testament congregations there were no professional ministers. No full-time clergy. Every member was a minister, and they shepherded each other.

It is five years since those first officers asked the congregation to join them in daily prayer. Working with human frailties, no system can be perfect. But because every person in our congregation is assigned to pray, this is a fact—I do not know of any church anywhere, any size, where a person-to-person ministry is any more effective.

We were seventy-five miles away conducting a Family Life Seminar. My wife and I do this often. Shortly after midnight the phone rang. Louis had died. Suddenly. For

eighty, he had been in wonderful health, so it was a shock to all of us. Of course, we dressed and went immediately. When we arrived, who do you think we found with Rachel? You're right. Her prayer partners had come to wait out the night with her.

Later we discovered this interesting fact. She called her prayer partners *first*. Before relatives, before the minister, she turned to them.

John and Betty Bryant are beautiful people. Libby is three and she has a baby brother on the way.

Any mother of a three-year-old needs to get out of the house now and then. Usually *now*. And shouldn't a pregnant woman have time with her husband alone? If you could observe what goes on at 259 Beachview, you would see the Bryants leave Libby with the Robinsons. They're going out for dinner, just John and Betty, to read each other's souls. And why have they driven twelve miles to bring their daughter here? The Robinsons are retired. They're not related to the Bryants, as we commonly think of relatives. But they *are* related. Prayer does do wonderful things for people. It draws together young couples and older couples. It makes warm friends of retired people and three-year olds.

Judy is about to have her baby. This is the first for Judy and Ken. Bob and Connie sit out the long drag with him.

Nothing unusual about friends sitting up with friends for an event like this. But these four people didn't even know each other a year ago. Now they're bound together in a very special way. They're prayer partners.

Two beautiful young couples are having a dinner tonight for a single lady. Dorothy is a retired woman, a most unusual person. She had once been food supervisor of a large chain of restaurants along an eastern turnpike. And would you believe these two couples are having a dinner especially for her! Reason? It's the end of the year. They are expressing their appreciation for twelve months of effective prayer partnership.

There are countless little scenes like this in our church. It isn't that everyone is turned on to the program. They're not. But here it is one more time—I don't know another church where so many small demonstrations of love are taking place daily.

I know churches with parish plans, buddy plans, zone plans, friendship plans. These are all movements in the right direction. I'm for anything which creates any kind of ministry. Yet I've been asked to examine dozens of these efforts, and I've studied them close up. Sad thing: the majority failed because they couldn't generate their own power.

Germane to the Christian faith is the belief that man

cannot save himself. Neither can he maintain genuine concern for the needs of others without divine help. Prayer alone produces steady care.

6

Where the People Pray—
Lives Will Be Changed

"My mom is so much easier to get along with since she got on this prayer kick."

Straight from a teenage daughter, reporting it like it is. Everyone knows mothers and daughters don't always have good vibes. But like the motto says, "Prayer changes things."

In any church where people pray there will be changes made. In the life of the church. In the spirit of the congregation. But especially, there will be changes in people.

When heart doors open to let the Lord in, he does what needs doing. Sometimes it's minor adjustments. Some-

times upheaval. He moves this person a little bit to the left, that one somewhat to the right. And some he turns completely around in the dramatic meaning of New Testament conversion.

Like the Nolens. Nobody would have guessed the sinister conflicts going on at their address. They looked so chic, so super-sophisticated. Mack was a superb provider. Why shouldn't he be on an executive salary like his? But they were in my study because things were coming unglued. Their teenage son was in serious trouble. And it appeared that his sister was headed in the same direction. Mack had been gone too much since his promotion. When he did come home, he was tired and short with Rosalie. Plus he was much too harsh with the children. Result? A family coming apart and a marriage bound for trouble.

The Nolens had been casual members in their former church. Attended some, pledged a little, but not really with it. They had shaken hands with their pastor at the door sometimes on Sunday. And that was about the extent of their personal contact.

Now in a church with prayer partners came the miracle. Enter the Fergusons. By any measurement, Stan and Lu are among the beautiful people. Young. Successful. Above all, lovers. They love each other. They love their children, and more than anything else, they love the Lord. They love the Lord with a practical, down-to-earth concern for other people born out of prayer.

If you were to talk to the Fergusons, they would tell you this is a new experience for them. They had never been challenged before to pray for those outside their own circle. Yet, the Nolens would tell you that Stan and Lu saved their home. To which Stan and Lu would immediately say, "It was the Lord. Not us."

At first Lu Ferguson and Rosalie Nolen met for coffee. Then out of their sharing across several weeks, Stan got next to Mack. Now the love of God had a channel.

Would that particular healing have happened anywhere else than in this church? Nobody knows. But we do know this—great things have happened also to the Owens and Johnsons, the McDermotts and Youngs. It has happened to people named Smith and Jones and many more.

You will understand immediately this isn't the case in every matching of prayer partners. All lives aren't touched so deeply. But here is a truth we've seen again and again. Prayer works miracles in human hearts. It does break through in amazing ways to change the lives of those who pray.

7

Where the People Pray—
They Attract New People

So prayer changes individuals. It has its effect on families. But this isn't all. Prayer creates its own image and makes the church more attractive to the outsider.

Many denominational efforts to evangelize are built on the assumption that the good guys are all "in here" and the lost are all "out there."

> So, you win the one next to you,
> And I'll win the one next to me.
> In no time at all,
> We'll have them all.
> Win them, win them,
> One by one.

To what?

To a big membership? To a beautiful building? Stained-glass windows? Cushions on the pews? Status? Activity?

If I read the signs right, this kind of evangelism is losing its drawing power. Today's sophisticated non-churchman is wising up to the same old pitches.

I've come across some unique evangelism efforts. Hard sell. Soft sell. Subtle. Specific. Some in a hurry. Some willing to wait. Phone calls. Home calls. Business calls. Some which smack of "You better or else." Others touching on superficial reasons to "come join us." Busing. Car pools. And I know a summer church where they even go in boats to bring them from miscellaneous resorts.

I'm not knocking any of these. Effective evangelism is of numerous kinds. But after many experiments, I'll take the evangelism of prayer.* This is one reason our big city church grew so rapidly. People would drive miles to join us. Why? Lots of reasons. But I believe they came mainly because they knew they'd be prayed for.

The same thing happens in our little church. People of different denominations come. They come from some distance for several reasons. But the best of the reasons is that prayer has drawing power of its own.

So there are numberless reasons why people join churches. But I think the reasons of tomorrow will be

---

*For information on the Evangelism Prayer Chain, Memorial Drive Church, Houston, Texas, see *How to Develop a Praying Church*, Charlie Shedd, Abingdon, 1964.

along the line of personal lay ministry. That's why I've concluded that prayer is the one best way to bring new people into the church.

Why?

Because prayer creates a church worth bringing people into.

8

Where the People Pray—
There Will Be Social Concern

"He was a champion of social justice. Preached some phase of it almost every Sunday. The only trouble was he didn't know how to get the people motivated. In fact, toward the end, the more he talked the more they sat on zero."

That is a verbatim quotation of a Presbyterian elder as he described his departing minister. But it could have been almost any other denomination.

Everywhere there are leaders like this . . . big on zeal but weak on inspiration. It is high time the church comes alive to community causes, national causes, the causes of justice for all. But it is readily apparent on every hand that things can go wrong here. Many a split congregation is still trying to heal these hurts. What seemed so right at first brought only confusion. And many a disillusioned minister heads for the exit, beat and bewildered.

From what I've seen, the most effective social ministry comes out of prayer. I've seen the task forces of a large praying church moving into the ghetto. I've seen Christian businessmen of prayer plan housing programs for depressed areas. And I've thrilled as I watched these people of upper-middle-class background do unusual things. Ministry in jails. Ministry to parolees. Ministry in juvenile court. All these in a big church where people prayed.

In a small congregation, same thing. Retired men fixing bicycles for the Boys' Club. Teens conducting a Valentine party at the saddest of nursing homes. Young couples bringing the poorest of the poor to their church for a party. Women volunteering in hospitals. Southern ladies ministering to people of every class and every color. I've seen courageous men risking their own security for the causes of ecology. And I know their courage came from their prayers.

So, what kind of mind does the Lord need for lighting his fires?

From what I've seen I'll take the praying mind, the praying layman, the clergyman at prayer. There will be a passion for justice in this kind of mind. But it will be tempered with good judgment.

9

Where the People Pray—
They Also Serve the Church

"Do you think I could be working so hard for the church that I've gotten out of touch with the Lord?"

That's what she asked. And I had to agree this was a definite possibility. Maxine was an expert at almost everything. Super efficient.

She had been asked to do this, serve on that committee, take charge here, be chairman there. And she had said "Yes." "Of Course." "Certainly."

Now she was spiritually dry. That's why she had come to her pastor's study.

Sometimes the church's problems come from people like Maxine who do too much and pray too little. But over here is a larger block who only sit. Taking up space is

their single contribution. In a praying church I've watched this imbalance work out. Some quit their running, quit wiping their fevered brow, quit trying to bring in the kingdom by themselves. Others who did nothing were moved from their inertia to take a place, serve a cause, do a job. And for every activity, I have found it easier to secure effective workers from praying people.

But as a pastor, I don't always know who needs to be accomplishing what. God alone knows that. And this is another good thing in a praying church—He brings his own balance when people are open to him.

Clergymen have this same need for balance. We probably aren't much busier than other people. We may think we are. But almost everyone these days has too much to do and too little time.

So with the pastor. Committees to organize. Calling. Meetings to attend. Sermon preparation. Money to raise. Hurt feelings. Emergencies. Hospitals to check. Bad news. Accidents. Weddings. Rehearsals. Death calls. Funerals. Counseling. Some we can help. Some too far out for us. Mimeographing. Sunday school. Boy Scouts. Girl Scouts. Denominational programs. Causes. Drives. Love that Jeremiah 9:2, "Oh that I had in the wilderness a lodging place of wayfaring men; that I might leave my people, and go from them!"

Meanwhile back at the parsonage our own children needing a father. And a wife wonders, "How much do I matter?"

What man on his own is big enough for all this? Nobody, I know. Which may be one more reason why so many are checking out, breaking down, or staying and suffering. So here's an observation from one who's run the gamut. I've been from little church to medium church, from medium church to big church. I've gone from big church to giant church and then back to little church again. In retrospect, I'm inclined to think that size doesn't matter all that much. A pastor can be harassed and harried among the masses. He can be harassed and harried with a handful. Or he can be at peace in either setting. And the difference is in his prayer life.

This has been my experience and this is my witness: The more time I spend in prayer, the better I do whatever needs doing for Him.

10

Where the People Pray—
They Reach Out to the World

Where people pray there will be an excitement about sharing the Good News. That ought to be standard equipment in every church which calls itself Christian. Our Lord said he wants all peoples and every nation for himself.

Why has the church failed to promote its mission effort? Sometimes the problem is lack of information. More often it is too small a goal, or rationalizations like: "We always meet our asking". . ."We're doing as well as anyone in our Conference". . ."As soon as we get the debt paid off, we intend to give more."

All of which is saying what? What it is saying really is that there is only a lukewarm interest. And the lukewarm interest can be traced to a lukewarm relationship with the Christ who said, "Go ye into all the world."

So what's to be done? One thing to be done is to get the people praying. Why? Lots of good reasons. But this has to be one of the best: where people pray, there will be new zeal for mission causes.

I have seen this result of prayer firsthand in two kinds of churches. I have watched it up close in a mammoth membership with dollar for dollar mission giving. Plus, I have seen prayer completely remake the giving attitudes of our little church at Jekyll Island. From recipients of mission support asking, "How much will we get this year?" I've watched this church turn 180 degrees. Today, if you could listen in on their discussions, you would hear some of them asking: "How soon can we move to matching our own dollars with a mission budget for others?"

I deal with this at greater length in another of the *Exciting Church* series. But right now, let's say it one more time: When people pray, the Lord comes in. When the Lord comes in, he generates excitement. When he generates excitement, there will be enough dollars for local work and places far away.

11

Where the People Pray— the Little Negatives Stay Little

I was about to congratulate myself on my new-found talent for keeping people happy. It disturbs me when I know they're complaining. Sharp tongues are not among my favorite things. I have some minister friends who say this never bothers them. But I wonder. Is this right? Even Jesus asked his disciples what the people were saying about him. So, I guess all this is somewhat normal. Wherever people gather, there will be talk, both positive and otherwise.

That's why I wanted to add this little note. When I became interested in prayer and moved my church in that direction, another fine thing happened. Much of the nit-picking seemed to subside. Why?

One practical answer is that prayer partners complain to their prayer partners. And sometimes surfacing little hostilities is all people need to get on with more important things.

12

Where the People Pray—
Everyone Is Able to Serve

Comes now another plus factor. Every person in the church who takes his prayer assignment seriously is contributing something vital. Some can't teach or don't want to. There are women who will never respond to the traditional ladies' auxiliary. Every church has men who could care less for the men's club. Some won't go for the couple's group, and others feel no need for church school, classes, study units. But everyone can pray. And whoever takes seriously his appointment knows he is of genuine importance to the Lord's work here.

In a church like this, shut-ins have a vital place. Removed from the main stream of worship and meetings, it is easy for them to feel left out. But when the most significant work of the church is prayer, they can be important too. Intercession does not need to be done under a spire with beautiful appointments on the altar. It can be done equally well in the home of a shut-in. It can also be done by those who do not take to regular church work.

III

Questions and Answers

Questions and Answers

As a neophyte at genuine prayer, I have needed all kinds of help. Still do. And one of my best sources through the years has been questions. Questions from correspondence, questions from meetings, a variety of questions from interested people. They keep me thinking. Probing. Some I've taken to my people for discussion. From a drawer full of questions, I have selected here those most frequently asked.

Why start with the officers?

QUESTION: Why begin with the officers? Couldn't we get going faster if we went straight to the congregation?

ANSWER: Yes, you could, but speed isn't the key. At first those few people in the congregation praying personally for others is all-important. They discuss it. Word gets around. If the leaders are talking, this gives the movement added impetus from the outset.

Starting in a group

QUESTION: Do you think this prayer trio organization could work for groups in the church?

ANSWER: Yes, it could. And it has. I know some youth groups where it's been effective. Also women. One pastor introduced it to his choir. They had been having internal difficulties so he asked them to draw names. He says it became a real blessing. I'm for starting wherever you can start and making it work wherever you can. Perhaps from one of these groups it can broaden to take in the whole congregation. But I still think the best place to start is with the officers.

Specifics on appointments

QUESTION: Will you be a little more specific about how you make appointments? Do you draw names? Use a chart? How do you do it? Sounds complicated.

ANSWER: We use a three by five card system. One card for each family. Then we begin to match cards. We shuffle, reshuffle, and shuffle some more until the whole thing seems to "feel" right. Actually, this isn't as complicated as it sounds. But it isn't done casually either. It takes time. By "we" I mean whoever is in charge of the groupings. This may be a man and wife, someone who knows the congregation well, the minister and his assistants.

Appointments at the worship service

QUESTION: You said your first appointments were made at a Family Night dinner. We only get our core people at these events. Any other suggestions?

ANSWER: Yes. Because we had the same experience, we found a better way. Appointments are made the first Sunday in February at morning worship. Cards are distributed. Names read and the trio comes forward to the communion table. Here they greet each other if they're acquainted. If they don't know each other, they are introduced before the congregation. Although this takes considerable time, it is really a beautiful service which seems to seal the importance of the people's prayers. In the case of larger churches this may take several Sundays.

Reason for "three"

QUESTION: Why trios? Wouldn't couples work just as well?

ANSWER: We think trios are better for several reasons. With couples, one might move, leaving the other alone. One could be unresponsive, which results in neglect for the other. But the main reason for three is the assurance of daily prayer for everyone. Suppose one member forgets or doesn't take it seriously, there are still two possibilities left that every member will be prayed for daily by someone. Also, in emergency needs, if one family is out of town or can't be reached, the other will likely be available.

"New" members

QUESTION: What do you do about new members who join during the year?

ANSWER: When new appointments are made, we create some pairs rather than trios to allow room for new members. Occasionally, as the year moves along and new people join, we break up a trio to rearrange the assignments. This kind of flexibility is one more plus in keeping the program workable.

QUESTION: What about the members who were in the church before your prayer partner program? Isn't it unfair to demand something altogether new from them? We're in an old church with a lot of long-time members. Do you exclude any of these from the prayer partners?

ANSWER: Our officers voted to make no exceptions. Everyone is included. In any church there will be defenders of the status quo. But an amazing thing will happen in some of these cases when the challenge is put to them. Certain of the old guard will respond. As one lady said, "I've been a church member for twenty-three years, and this is the first time I've been asked to do something I think is significant." Others now sense a genuine love going out from their lives and coming back to them. For some, this is a new and thrilling experience. So I wouldn't worry unduly here. Some may gradually fade away but more will be turned on like they've never been turned on before.

Rancor within the group

QUESTION: Our church has a long history and some of it pretty hairy. You know how it is, people who don't get along. Has this ever happened to you? I mean did this ever get in the way with prayer partner appointment?

ANSWER: Occasionally, we make appointments where people don't seem to blend. Some of these have been potentially embarrassing. Unknown to us at the time, unpleasant things have happened in the past between families. There might conceivably be situations in local churches where reshuffling is necessary. We've never done it that way. And because we haven't, there have been some real miracles. We learned very early that this is possible. Two families who had negative feelings for each other were placed in the same trio. We learned of it, because they told us later. They also said their initial thought was to ask for reappointment. But after doing a retake, they decided to let it stand. And they reported some positive healing of memories. Friendships replacing rancor are nothing unusual in our congregation. It isn't that someone is clever at patching up wounds. It is because the Lord has a way of easing the hurts of his children when people pray.

The inactives and those who won't get with it

QUESTION: What do you do with a member who contributes or attends but wants no part of the prayer program? Also we have a lot of inactives who are members in name only. Any advice about these?

ANSWER: Where the emphasis is on prayer as the most important aspect of the church, these things gradually take care of themselves. Those who want no part of it will phase out.

              In our church the current policy is, "This is a church where everyone is prayed for every day by someone." Membership is open to those who will participate on this basis.

              That statement is made public. And the membership tends to move either toward this reality or away from it. Our leaders do not carry a hatchet or conduct witch hunts.

              Inactives in our particular congregation are placed on the "suspended" roll if they fail to meet certain standards. Churches without such standards will need a policy set by the officers.

Widows and young people

QUESTION: In our church we have a lot of widows. We also have some children and young people whose parents aren't members. What do you recommend we do about this when appointments are made?

ANSWER: You've touched on a very important point, because this would be true in almost every church. At first we made an attempt to put widows with widows and single children with single children. Then one year we began to vary it. And much to our surprise, we found it added a lot to put single children with families, widows with couples.

Notifying

QUESTION: Do you notify the prayer partners in emergencies like hospitalization, accident, death, and other things?

ANSWER: Yes. I see myself as pastor to the entire congregation. But in our case, each member also has a real pastoral ministry to his prayer partners. I notify prayer partners of special needs. And I ask them to call me. Many of them do. In a praying group, there will be fewer neglected needs because genuine concern is generated by prayer.

The single commitment

QUESTION: Do you ask your prayer partners to meet regularly for prayer?

ANSWER: No. We ask for only one commitment: daily prayer. Some of them do get together to pray about particular needs. But that's their idea, not ours. Underlying all we do is the emphasis, "You pray, and the Spirit will lead you to what's right for you and your prayer partners."

Larger churches

QUESTIONS: You have described a program in a small church, but we have a thousand members. Will it work for us?

We have two thousand members. Do you see any complications because of our size?

ANSWER: Size always brings complexity, and the more people, the more complications. When our church in Houston, Texas, went over two thousand members, we added a membership secretary who kept all the records. She was in daily contact with the program and its needs. A number of volunteer workers assisted her. But there was no question about the value of all this effort to the large church. Rule: The larger the congregation, the more important a daily ministry to every person.

Opposition

QUESTION: In our church there are three or four leaders who automatically vote against anything new. We have tried several times to start something different, but it gets voted down in the board. How do you handle problems like this?

ANSWER: The only way to circumvent such a bottleneck is by majority rule and the secret ballot. Of course, if your pastor is afraid of these people, you've had it. If he will not let the majority rule you need a new pastor or new officers. But where he will take the lead, the secret ballot (anonymous, unsigned) may get things moving in spite of opposition.

When the pastor drags his feet

QUESTION: What can you do when your minister is drag-
            ging his feet? I don't like to say this, but I
            think our minister is the main problem.
            Maybe he's afraid of some things which
            might happen. He pretends to be interested
            and talks that way, but I don't think he really
            is. Any suggestions?

ANSWER: Except to pray for him and tell him how you
            feel, I don't believe there is much you can
            do. I know some churches where certain
            types of prayer programs have been started
            in spite of the minister. But to develop an
            effective work where the minister is disinter-
            ested or undercutting is a near impossibility.

Testing place

QUESTION: Prayer movements sometimes lead to unfamiliar things. Dangerous kinds of faith healing, hysterical forms of glossolalia, or even a split in the church. How can we be sure these things won't happen? Is there any way to safeguard the program?

ANSWER: The Bible gives us a good testing place. Galatians 5:22–23 says, "The fruit of the Spirit is love, joy, peace," and a lot of other good things. One reason for divisions is a "holier than thou" attitude. This often results when people feel they have been exclusively tuned in to the Lord. But against Galatians 5:22 –23 that can't be authentic.

As a minister of a praying church, I've experienced very little of the negative in either large congregation or small. And I think there's a reason. When there is a prayer program, involving every member, there will be love and understanding. There will be tolerance and flexibility. Building a program on daily prayer often prevents those things which lead to dissension.

The small group movement and prayer partners

QUESTION: Our denomination is very big on small groups. We have several of them in our church and others starting. Some of these aren't very effective, but others really do a lot of good. As I hear you describe prayer partners, I wonder if you're talking about the same thing as small groups. Or would they be in opposition to each other? Is there room in a church for both?

ANSWER: The small group movement is a welcome new breeze blowing across the church in our land. I'm glad for small groups. I've had them in large churches, middle-size churches, little churches. I've met with them in countless settings on many themes. I'm an enthusiastic supporter of the small group movement. But no matter how effective they've been, the facts are they have touched only a limited number even in churches known for their group work. So here is another argument for the prayer partner program. Every member is part of a small group for prayer and concern.

True, it is not a structured development in

the same meaning as most small group programs. But I see no reason to consider the two movements as opposed to each other. In our little congregation we have several small groups. In a real sense daily prayer makes people want to meet together, study together, enjoy each other. Experience shows that these desires are always prompted when people open their hearts daily to the Lord.

Twenty-four hour vigils and special calls to prayer

QUESTIONS: We have a twenty-four hour prayer vigil every year during Holy Week. Someone is at the
church every hour, praying. We ask people
to sign up, and we never have trouble getting
volunteers. What do you think of this?

Our preacher recently asked us all to pray
for world peace whenever we stop at a red
light. Is this a good thing?

The canvas committee this year suggested
that everyone in the church pray at 5:00
o'clock in the afternoon about the budget
and pledges. Why they picked 5:00, I don't
know, except maybe that's when most of us
get off work. I'm kind of wondering whether
this does much good. What do you think?

ANSWER: Every special effort which brings people to
pray probably has some merit. But here are
two basic questions for any prayer program:

A. Does it lead to ongoing regular prayer?
B. Does it place the responsibility on all
   members alike?

Undershepherds

QUESTION: I read your book, *How to Develop a Praying Church.* You describe there how your church was organized around the "Undershepherds." Is this prayer program you're talking about now the same thing?

ANSWER: No. In the prayer partner program every member of the church is asked to assume a prayer partner responsibility. The book to which you refer describes a development where one-third of the church members were praying for the other two-thirds.

Make it your own

QUESTION: Who can we find to come to our church and give us a pep talk about all this?

ANSWER: Maybe you shouldn't import anyone. It might be better to work it out on your own. One more time—I'd begin with the officers. This gives it a solid footing you wouldn't get from an outsider. And I would carefully guard against saying, "We know a church which does things this way." Don't worry about giving credit. The Bible says, "There is no new thing under the sun." I'd lay it on the hearts of your own people until it comes fresh and new from them.

IV

Questions on the
Special Needs Prayer Chain

Questions on the Special Needs Prayer Chain

The Special Needs Prayer Chain is an important adjunct to the prayer partner program in our little church at Jekyll Island. It was and is also a major feature of the prayer program at Memorial Drive Church in Houston.

Space does not permit thorough treatment of all the ramifications. Yet everywhere I go particular questions keep surfacing. Following are those most frequently asked.

Beginning

QUESTION: How would you start a Special Needs Prayer Chain? I mean, will you take it from the beginning as if your church had never heard of anything like this?

ANSWER: First, I'd bring some folks together who are interested in prayer. A handful will do. They should be sensitive people with sympathetic hearts. I'd ask them for a commitment to pray. Then I'd make an announcement to the congregation, "We have a new group in the church who are willing to pray for special needs." Next, I'd give out a number to call. Now wait. It won't be long.

Getting organized

QUESTION: How do you organize for a work like this?

ANSWER: To begin with I'd have one group. I'd make a list of the chairman and each member. The name of the chairman is frequently announced (or published in the bulletin) and people soon learn to call this number. Or they might call the pastor.

Each member of the chain is then called in this manner: Number one calls number two, two calls three, etc., until the entire chain has received the message within a few minutes.

When the chain grows beyond ten people, it's better to make two groups. Our current chain is divided into four units each with its own chairman. When the general chairman is called, he calls each subchairman and the request is called on down. If the person next in line isn't available, he skips that name and calls the next. (Then it's his responsibility to call his regular later.)

How long?

QUESTION: When a request comes, how long do you keep it on the Special Needs Prayer Chain?

ANSWER: One week. On the seventh day prayer chain members release the request. The group studies how this can be done. But each individual commits the person to the Lord in his own way.

Some people may be prayed for longer, but this is because the request is repeated.

How much knowledge?

QUESTION: One group we studied only wants initials. They also prefer not to know details about a situation. How does your group handle this?

ANSWER: We use names, and we also feel that the more we know, the more effective we can be.

Some intercessors say that too much negative input is detrimental to prayer. With us the more total the picture, the more totally we're able to relate it to the total love of God.

"Special"?

QUESTION: Doesn't it seem presumptuous for some people to set themselves up as special? I mean,
aren't they inferring they are righteous
enough to pray for others?

ANSWER: This possibility is frequently brought up, but
we've never had problems with it. Nor do I
think it's something to worry about. This
group does not set themselves up as special
people or as better than anyone else. Rather,
they are people willing to pray for special
needs. When a person prays regularly, he
measures himself not against others, but
against the Lord. If they aren't humble at the
outset, this kind of praying will soon make
them that way.

Gossip?

QUESTION: Do you have any problem with people talk-
            ing too much? Aren't some of the things you
            pray about confidential? How do you handle
            the busybody or the gossip?

ANSWER: This is another question asked at every Pray-
            er Seminar I conduct.

            We have never had a problem with this ei-
            ther. Which says something about the kind
            of people who are doing the praying. Even
            if someone joined the chain with impure
            motives, I believe they would soon be puri-
            fied by genuine praying.

Healing?

QUESTION: Do you always pray for healing? Isn't it true that God knows better than we do how things ought to be?

ANSWER: You're right. We often receive calls like this from a frantic daughter. "Mother is having an operation tomorrow. I'm calling everyone I can think of to pray that it won't be malignant. She just has to be all right."

This is a natural reaction in crisis. So we don't argue. People in their crises are not looking for lessons in theology. We take the name and pray in our own way. And our own way is to pray without giving God a blueprint.

Christians believe in miracles. Christians believe in healing. But Christians also know that God's ways are more wonderful than our ways. So the theology of our praying is in this direction: We know that God loves them. We pray that they might feel his love right now and respond to it. We ask that they might grasp the scope of God's love. Miracles sometimes include death with a resurrection we can't see. We ask also that all might remember the eternal aspects of divine healing.

Stories of Miracles?

QUESTION: I suppose you have some stories you could
tell us about miracles from your prayer
chain work. Would you mind sharing some
of these?

ANSWER: Yes, some amazing things have been reported. And we know many of these firsthand.
But we never talk about them. And the rea·
son is this kind of talk soon becomes distort-
ed. It gets built up into a kind of magic. God
alone knows what's a miracle. So we pray
and leave the miracle to him. Any group
which begins a work like this will soon experience some startling things, some puzzling
things. But the main emotion is one of grat-
itude that God is good and his love is far
greater than our little minds can fathom.

In and Out?

QUESTION: Are people allowed to drop out of the Special Needs Prayer Chain? I sense this work could get wearisome. Also won't people get the feeling this is a closed little group?

ANSWER: Anyone can excuse himself from this service any time, but very few do.

New prayer chain members are invited from the pulpit frequently. Our chairman right now is a young mother who looks like a high schooler. Quarterly the group gets together for discussion and study. Prior to each of these meetings, this charming young woman comes before the congregation to extend an invitation. Often people who have been on the receiving end will now accept her invitation.

Variations for the large church

QUESTION: Can you tell us about effective variations to the approach you have described?

ANSWER: Yes. Let me tell you how they do it today at Memorial Drive Presbyterian in Houston, Texas. That church, which now has a membership of over five thousand, continues a major emphasis on prayer. Because there are so many people interested, they have divided their Special Needs Prayer Chain into seven groups, one for each day of the week. Calls coming in on Monday are referred to the Monday group. Tuesday calls to that group. This prevents big lists from becoming burdensome. And it also expedites the rapid handling of requests.

Each church would do well to consider the needs of its particular congregation. Then adapt the entire program to care for those needs.

My wife has an expression which blesses my soul. When I reach for the moon, push too hard for success, or become discouraged for lack of response, she will ask, "Aren't you trying to out-Jesus Jesus?"

What she means, of course, is that he lost one out of twelve. Plus, there were many who drifted off, and others failed to respond in any way.

"Patience" is the key word in developing a local church prayer program. It may take several years to make the dream come true. But since the years are sure to pass anyway, here's an encouraging word from a North Carolina Baptist layman. His church has recently begun a prayer partner program.

"I'd say only 50 percent of our people are really with it after twelve months. But maybe we should simply thank God for that. That's 50 percent more than would have been praying without this challenge."

Other books by Charlie W. Shedd